THIS JOURNAL BELONGS TO

I AM A

SUN

MOON

VENUS

This edition first published in 2025 by Red Wheel, an imprint of
Red Wheel/Weiser, LLC
With offices at:
65 Parker Street, Suite 7
Newburyport, MA 01950
www.redwheelweiser.com

ISBN: 978-1-59003-582-5

Library of Congress Cataloging-in-Publication Data available upon request.

Design and illustrations by Belén Rigou and Chikovnaya via Creative Market
Typeset in Crimson Text

Printed in China
WM
10 9 8 7 6 5 4 3 2 1

SELF-LOVE ASTROLOGY
JOURNAL

AGUSTINA MALTER TERRADA

Red Wheel

CONTENTS

HOW TO USE THIS JOURNAL

Self-Love Astrology Journal will align your purpose with the universal pulse. To walk down this path, you will need to take the first step and plant the seeds along the way.

Chapter 1 gives you the tools to interpret your own natal chart. The zodiac has twelve phases: the signs. Recording them step by step will help you sync with the stars, explained in chapter 2. To deepen that connection, there are twelve rituals, actions that add meaning to your life. Put them into practice to focus your intentions and attract new energies. That is what we mean by "walking down the path."

If you want to spontaneously connect to these universal pulses, it is ideal to follow the zodiac calendar. For example, it's natural to feel ready to start when the Aries season begins. But this is not mandatory. The path begins whenever this journal finds you.

If you get stuck in the middle, don't feel bad. You may resume your path whenever your mind, body, or heart tells you to. The ideal path is in an upward spiral, but each chapter has its own frequency. This will grant you the freedom, for example, to start with phase 4, if you need a more intimate contact with yourself, and jump to phase 7 if you need to regain balance.

Reaching your purpose is living in the oasis. Chapter 3 gives you the opportunity to look back on the road taken and get ready for what is coming.

Do you trust the universe?

Mara Parra and Victoria Benaim
FERA
@fera.design

ACKNOWLEDGMENTS

I never knew where I was heading, yet I reached the oasis. I want to thank myself for that intuition.

This journey started unintentionally. Like astrology, this book was an experience that found me, not the other way around. I thank a Higher Power for sending me signs and wonderful people at key moments. I'm even thankful for the obstacles I ran into, as they helped me learn to choose what to keep and where to stay.

My mother is one of those inspiring people. When I told her I wanted to be an astrologer, she didn't say, "You're crazy." My siblings were there for me on all my journeys. My nieces and nephews helped me open to love again. Thank you, Manu, who I found around the corner and who filled my life with life. Each of my students, eager to learn, encouraged me to share my world. Those people who came to me with the excuse of having their natal chart read also taught me how to strengthen my purpose. I learn from everyone who finds inspiration in what I write. Thank you, Claudia, great woman and seer, who accompanied my healing process. And my dad, as he gave me room to be a free soul.

Special thanks to Mandarina, Locoto, and Flaco, my guides on Earth. They give me pure happiness in return for nothing other than food, walks, and toys.

Thanks to FERA for betting on me and granting me total freedom in this creative process.

And thank you, because this journal found you.

Agustina Malter Terrada

Only those who can tolerate the desert manage to reach the oasis.

— FEDERICO PERALTA RAMOS, AQUARIUS

CROSSING THE DESERT

I have always been captivated by the image of the desert. An endless number of grains of sand forming an austere sea, silent and cruel, where only what is essential sprouts and grows.

That's what the process of writing this book felt like. It was a way of getting to the essence of my workshop experience, where I shared with many others my love for astrology and where I realized that one cannot give what one doesn't have.

I learned that I can't write about something that is not inside me and that form and content are interrelated. A journal can help us approach mystery and make collective empowerment possible in the way that a map helps you cross the desert, even through sandstorms and mirages. I choose to realize what is possible, what is honest, what I can share based on my own experience. The rest is for you to find out for yourself. The oasis awaits you. It is dormant inside you.

CHAPTER 1

DISCOVERING THE SEED

Basic Notions and Natal Chart

CHAPTER 1

ASTROLOGY FOR SELF-LOVE

Astrology is a powerful ancient language that helps us connect the facts of our lives to the totality of which we are part. We all wonder about the reasons behind the events in our lives. Is there a plan?

Astrologers study the microcosm as a reflection of the whole universe. Physically, astrology derives from the movement of stars, and although it is neither science nor religion, it uses a method of interpretation. Every cosmic movement has implications for our planet. For example, a full Moon is a body that generates certain energies on Earth and in the human psyche. Any sentient being can experience this.

This is an empowering tool because it gives us back responsibility: in each of us is all the information of who we are. We forget this when we are born, but we can recover it. This is the mystery. Instead of wondering why, we need to turn our life into a big *what for*.

More than anything, astrology is love. We need to develop empathy into a kind of consciousness that loves discovering more than achieving, and learning more than mastering. Without love (of ourself and others), there is no destiny we can face, no relationship we can heal.

Allow life to transform you and enjoy the journey of self-love. Embrace this journal.

THE EVOLUTION OF ASTROLOGY

It is believed that astrology was born in the third millennium BCE. Seeking to answer the question of what we are doing here on Earth, people began to think about the relationship between the stars and Earth. It came even before religion. It is a cosmic thread that is still followed today.

ANCIENT WORLD

It all started in Chaldea (a country that was located in what is now southern Iraq). It was then used by the Egyptians, Romans, Greeks, and Chinese. Back then, astrology was basically a predictive system.

MIDDLE AGES

Christianity felt threatened by the practice of any world-view that did not follow the sacred scriptures. Astrology was considered witchcraft and was forced to survive underground.

RENAISSANCE

The light of reason placed the Sun in the center of the system. Astronomy became strong. The old sisters split apart: astrology and astronomy each went their own way.

MODERNITY

Scientific advances led to the discovery of new planets, namely Uranus, Neptune, and Pluto. This updated the astrological knowledge.

TODAY

In the 21st century, the current paradigm is linked and universal. We use astrology as a self-knowledge tool. Its therapeutic focus is placed on the client.

KEY CONCEPTS

SYNCHRONICITY

What happens on the outside is connected to what we perceive internally. There is no such thing as chance. When everything "fits," it's because the conscious and subconscious levels are aligned. For example, I want to travel to China, and a Chinese restaurant opens on my street.

VIBRATION

Everything is vibrating; nothing is still. We are interactive, resonating frequencies. In the universe, everything moves at different energetic levels.

POLARITY

Everything is made of pairs of opposites. Opposites are identical in nature but different in degree. Extremes can touch. Cold and hot are different states of the same thing: temperature. In the same way, Gemini and Sagittarius are different states of the same relationship.

ARCHETYPES

Images loaded with sensitive and symbolic meaning work as ideal models for things. Archetypes are the substance of the collective unconscious. For example, the maternal archetype is the universal image of what a mother should be.

CORRESPONDENCE

The principle reads: "As above, so below." We say there is correspondence when we can see the reflection of an inner aspect projected on something external, and vice versa.

COLLECTIVE UNCONSCIOUS

This is a set of ancient universal memories. All the archetypes of humanity live in the unconscious. An example of this is our ancestral fear of darkness.

ENERGY TO BEGIN

1. Pay attention to the way this journal came into your hands. Can you link this experience to any of the key concepts on the previous page?

2. Write down three sentences that describe you today.

3. How do you think that astrology can help you?

4. Paste a picture of yourself on this page. Write down the date. You will understand the significance of this by the end of the book.

   Date:

NATAL CHART

The natal chart is the relationship between who you are (identity) and what happens to you (destiny).

You can think of it as a compass, guiding you to get to know yourself better. It is a great tool for foreseeing energetic contexts and understanding how to navigate life.

The natal chart represents the position of stars at the moment of your birth. It is calculated using the date and exact time and place where you were born. You can think of it as a living picture of the sky in that moment: your celestial DNA. All natal charts together make up a great network of relationships.

The natal mandala represents the link between heaven and Earth. Inside it, the chart is divided into twelve portions called houses. They represent the earthly plane. On the outer circumference, we have the zodiac wheel made of the twelve signs, representing the sky. The houses may change size, but the zodiac doesn't: each sign is 30 degrees wide, and the total wheel is 360 degrees.

Take a look at the position of houses and planets in Taylor Swift's chart.

The ascendant, or rising sign, is the energy growing on the horizon at the moment of your birth. The ascendant marks the beginning of the first house, organizing the rest of the zodiac on the chart. The planets are placed in the houses and tell us how their function is manifested through certain experiences. In addition, they are imbued with the vibration of the sign they are placed in.

The solar return is the annual natal chart, starting on each birthday and calculated based on the Sun's return to its position on the day you were born. The solar return shows a new cycle that allows the unfolding of different innate qualities.

TAYLOR SWIFT'S NATAL CHART

Born December 13, 1989, 8:36 a.m., in Reading, Pennsylvania

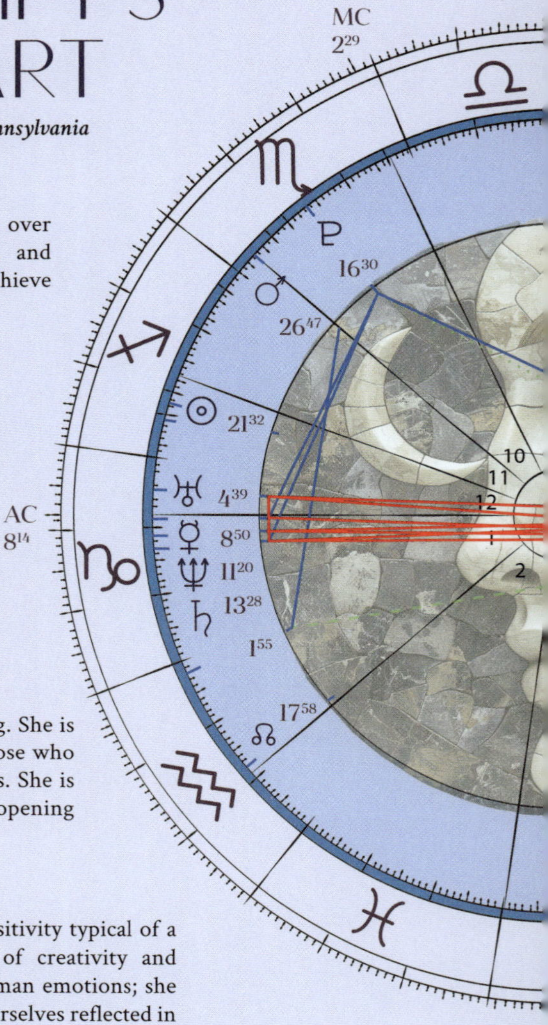

Capricorn Ascendant

Taylor is capable of sustaining her dreams over time through hard work, determination, and discipline. Life puts her to the test. She can achieve success and recognition on a large scale.

Stellium in Capricorn

With so many planets in this sign, it is important for her to always keep trying and never give up. In her own words, "I could build a castle out of all the bricks they threw at me." She came into this world to create her own rules. She did not follow in her father's footsteps; he was a successful banker, and she chose to be an artist.

Sun in Sagittarius

She is adventurous, optimistic, and outgoing. She is a natural leader who touches the lives of those who allow themselves to be touched by her lyrics. She is generous in sharing her experiences and opening her heart.

Sun in the Twelfth House

This position predicts a magnetism and sensitivity typical of a leader. Taylor moves in an atmosphere of creativity and invisible connections; her songs capture human emotions; she acts as a channel. Her light allows us to see ourselves reflected in her personal universe.

Moon in Cancer

She has the ability to provide protection but also to be vulnerable. She shows intimacy typical of poets and artists. Her inspirational material comes from her own experiences of love and heartbreak and from her family roots (such as her relationship with her grandmother, who was a famous opera singer). She also loves cats and declares herself a proud cat lady.

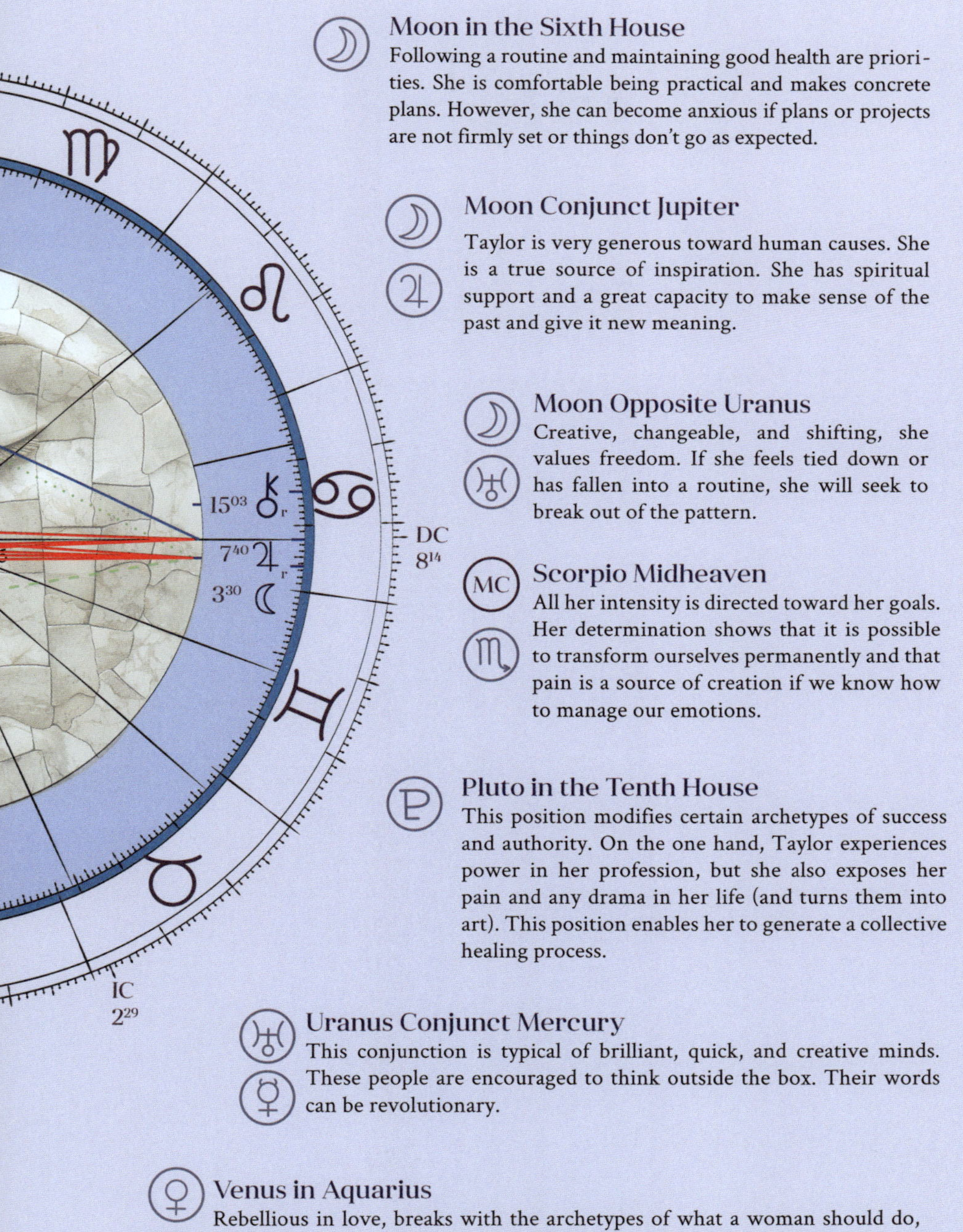

Moon in the Sixth House

Following a routine and maintaining good health are priorities. She is comfortable being practical and makes concrete plans. However, she can become anxious if plans or projects are not firmly set or things don't go as expected.

Moon Conjunct Jupiter

Taylor is very generous toward human causes. She is a true source of inspiration. She has spiritual support and a great capacity to make sense of the past and give it new meaning.

Moon Opposite Uranus

Creative, changeable, and shifting, she values freedom. If she feels tied down or has fallen into a routine, she will seek to break out of the pattern.

Scorpio Midheaven

All her intensity is directed toward her goals. Her determination shows that it is possible to transform ourselves permanently and that pain is a source of creation if we know how to manage our emotions.

Pluto in the Tenth House

This position modifies certain archetypes of success and authority. On the one hand, Taylor experiences power in her profession, but she also exposes her pain and any drama in her life (and turns them into art). This position enables her to generate a collective healing process.

Uranus Conjunct Mercury

This conjunction is typical of brilliant, quick, and creative minds. These people are encouraged to think outside the box. Their words can be revolutionary.

Venus in Aquarius

Rebellious in love, breaks with the archetypes of what a woman should do, believes in the equality of genders, species, and beings. Values diversity.

ELEMENTS

Elements constitute the essence of the universe and tell us about the diverse ways of perceiving reality. They are the first thing one sees when analyzing a natal chart.

FIRE: I LIGHT

The Fire signs are **Aries**, **Leo**, and **Sagittarius**. If you get close to them, they'll keep you warm—or they will burn you. Fire is expressive, dramatic, spiritual, and desiring. This sign is interested in going on adventures and finding out if life is up to its epic imagination.

AIR: I THINK

The Air signs are **Gemini**, **Libra**, and **Aquarius**. Air represents thought and the mind. It is options, intelligence, speed, bonds, creativity, adaptability, and movement. Air likes to debate, theorize, and connect.

EARTH: I TOUCH

The Earth signs are **Taurus**, **Virgo**, and **Capricorn**. They have to do with the earthly realm. Earth is interested in evaluating reality and observing the position of things. Earth is concrete, stable, loyal, and undergoes slow, steady processes.

WATER: I FEEL

The Water signs are **Cancer**, **Scorpio**, and **Pisces**. Water represents feelings and emotions. It is affection, empathy, transmutation, and healing. Water seeks to share and merge its sensitivity with others. Water people are experts in intuition and resonance.

To put the theory of elements into practice, go to page 30.

- **Water** and **Earth** have receptive energy. Their direction is inward.
- **Fire** and **Air** have active energy. Their direction is outward.
- **Air** and **Water** are complementary opposites.
- **Earth** and **Fire** are complementary opposites.

THE TWELVE HOUSES

Houses represent the earthly plane. They are the concrete experiences in life. Each house describes specific scenarios that can give you information about who you are. You go through the houses to develop your consciousness.

FIRST HOUSE, OR ASCENDANT

The way you are perceived by others. It's the energy you use to start processes. By definition, you have no experience in this field. Your challenge is to become aware of it.

SECOND HOUSE

The resources that allow you to satisfy your needs. Your system of values. How you generate income.

THIRD HOUSE

Your ability to communicate. Short trips and relocation. The energy brought by your friends and family.

FOURTH HOUSE

The ability to connect to your own emotions. Your relationship with your mother. Where you come from and how you create a home.

FIFTH HOUSE

Your personal expression. The energy that identifies you. The talents you share with the world.

SIXTH HOUSE

Your practical world. Routines, health, self-care. The systems you are part of. The energy through which you feel useful.

SEVENTH HOUSE

Your relationships. The energy that complements you. The qualities you deny in yourself and project on others.

EIGHTH HOUSE

Your subconscious. Sexuality, your relationship to the occult, death, and processes of transformation.

NINTH HOUSE

Your philosophy and search for meaning. Exploration, travel, and learning. Your worldview.

TENTH HOUSE

Your profession and occupations. Goals, achievements, your relationship with your father, authority, and law. Social acknowledgment.

ELEVENTH HOUSE

Your role in friendships and community. Your contribution to the collective consciousness. Group creativity.

TWELFTH HOUSE

Your inner world. Spirituality, solitude, unexplored potential. The collective unconscious.

THE TWELVE SIGNS

The twelve signs represent subtle energetic qualities rather than distinct personality types. It's important to note that there is no person who is purely one sign. We all have the presence of the twelve zodiac energies in our natal chart in different proportions. The challenge is to transcend the idea of impenetrable categories and embrace the merging of these cosmic qualities.

♈ ARIES (March 21 – April 20)

Pioneers. They are brave, impulsive, relentless, and dynamic. They fight for their lives. Don't get in their way. They know how to release their fury and are not afraid to yell to settle things. Don't take it personally; this too shall pass.

♉ TAURUS (April 20 – May 21)

True children of nature. They are sensual and trust their feelings to help them satisfy their desires. They are natural providers. They may take their time to make decisions, exploring all options first. Once they choose a direction, don't try to make them change lanes.

♊ GEMINI (May 21 – June 21)

Bridges between distant points. They are spontaneous, multifaceted characters, loquacious people who love words. Their enemy is doubt, which can rob them of their power. They are afraid to choose because they don't want to be left without options. They know how to play the game of life. Their gift is communication.

♋ CANCER (June 21 – July 22)

Caretakers of the planet. They are sensitive, gentle, and nostalgic people who may feel the past was always better. They can be fearful of the future and the changes brought about by growing up. They protect the vulnerable and cherish the idea of home and intimate connections.

♌ LEO (July 23 – August 22)

Masters of self-love and confidence. They are authentic, uninhibited, and expressive. Their goal is to be as true to themselves as they can. They discourage imitators but still take credit for what they generate in others. They may value image more than intimacy.

♍ VIRGO (August 23 – September 22)

Organized and practical. They love systems and everything that follows logical order. The way things work is marvelous to them. Being able to improve those things is their divine gift. Virgos pay attention to detail, because they know the whole lies in every part. Their taste and love of beauty are unmatched.

♎ LIBRA (September 23 – October 23)

Keepers of balance and harmony. They find it hard to choose because they can see all sides. Their talent lies in their ability to negotiate. They know the truth is a bit here and a bit there, that everything that is beautiful has something ugly in it, and vice versa. Justice is finding points in common.

♏ SCORPIO (October 22 – November 22)

Masters of transformation. They know darkness and how to turn the lights on in the deep. They love to give, even if giving equals dying. They are existentialist and intense. Their possessiveness and control may stem from a fear of suffering. They also know how to heal and change skins to let power emerge from their own sensitivity and intuition.

♐ SAGITTARIUS (November 22 – December 21)

Universal explorers. They are expansive, abundant, and full of understanding. There are no borders in their heart, only a direct passport to the universe. They transmit their wisdom, educate, and inspire. Sometimes they are too idealistic and that prevents them from really consolidating their confidence in life.

♑ CAPRICORN (December 22 – January 20)

Paradigms of perseverance. The task is hard, but they are patient and methodical. They know how to tell the essential from the distraction. They know how to construct boundaries, and they know about frustration. When they are not comparing themselves against external models, they can be true experts at enabling the experience for others.

♒ AQUARIUS (January 20 – February 19)

True originals. They work for the common good, and visions of utopia help them stay grounded. Once they have learned to materialize them, their visions turn into real collective causes. They are creative, eccentric, and rebellious. They love freely and openly, with no fear of opposition.

♓ PISCES (February 19 – March 20)

Beautiful dreamers. Empathy, compassion, and symbiosis enable them to swim in diverse oceans, though they may need to drown a few times while learning these skills. Leaving the role of victim behind enables them to grow into healing beings. These soul artists vibrate in a very rare frequency: total love.

Note: The date ranges for each sign are estimates, because the Sun does not change signs on the same date every year. The sign change occurs on the cut-off date. For example, if you were born on March 20, depending on the hour of your birth, you could be either a Pisces or an Aries. This is determined by your detailed natal chart.

This concept is called *cusp*. Those who are born on transitional days (which may be a range of up to six days) will have the energy of both signs. In this journal, you will find two cusp women on the Taurus and Libra pages (pages 34 and 40). Yes! And the creator of this book also has this kind of energy.

THE PLANETS

The planets are concrete forces within the system. You can think of them as verbs that are modulated by the energy of the sign they are embedded in.

THE SUN

Essence. In the Sun, you are the center of your universe. Its light illuminates the central purpose of your life. Without it, there is no brightness in your system. You may feel a lack of motivation and be off your axis. The Sun also represents self-awareness that—if not refined—becomes pure ego, image, and mannerism. Your Sun sign colors your style.

* **Verbs:** Being, expressing, representing.

If your Sun is in Sagittarius, you say, "I'm a Sagittarius."

THE MOON

Feeling. The Moon is your protective membrane. Through its receptive energy, you can be in touch with positive emotions but also with fear. If your inner child's whims take over, the Moon will make you offer defensive, childish responses. The function of the Moon colors your way of giving and receiving affection.

* **Verbs:** Feeling, nurturing, caring.

If your Moon is in Taurus, you may need material stability to feel safe.

MERCURY

Communication. Mercury represents your way of reasoning and your ability to communicate. It encourages you to open to experiences, and it rules your way of learning. In Mercury, first you think, then you exist. Analysis and association of ideas are among its tasks. Mercury's function is to bridge the gap. The sign where Mercury is placed speaks about what interests you and arouses your curiosity.

* **Verbs:** Think, analyze, communicate.

If your Mercury is in Leo, you speak authentically from your heart and make yourself heard.

Have you ever heard about Mercury in retrograde? Look it up on page 25.

VENUS

Love. Venus is the force that moves you to find otherness. It speaks about your ability to love, choose, share, complement, and experience joy. If you cultivate your natal Venus, you are doing things to love yourself. In your natal chart, the sign where Venus is placed represents what you feel attracted to and the way you open to that.

* **Verbs:** Open, embellish, enjoy.

If your Venus is in Gemini, you like talking and communicating, and you feel attracted by intelligence.

MARS

Conquest. You need to reach out to life, and Mars grants you the required aggression. It represents your desire, whatever motivates you to emerge from the protective womb. You open your path through action, setting up your territory and using your body to confront. The sign where Mars is placed represents your level of energy and dynamism.

* **Verbs:** Activate, wish, defend.

If your Mars is in Pisces, you are motivated by what is subtle, and your actions are inspiring.

JUPITER

Expansion. Believing is creating. Jupiter is in charge of expanding the system beyond its known borders. As a master who leaves you thinking, Jupiter's wisdom arouses your curiosity. This planet reveals your ideals and what you open your mind to. The sign where your Jupiter is placed represents how you will open to your spiritual plan on Earth.

* **Verbs:** Expand, trust, direct.

If your Jupiter is in Cancer, you trust your emotions to guide your progress.

* **Cycle:** Jupiter spends a year in each sign, and it takes twelve years to complete the zodiac.

SATURN

Boundaries. Saturn's function within the system is to put your essential abilities to the test. It speaks about your ability to define, materialize, and sustain. Saturn determines what is possible and the limitations of earthly experiences. The sign where your Saturn is placed represents the obstacles that will help you grow.

* **Verbs:** Mature, essentialize, sustain.

If your Saturn is in Scorpio, you mature through crises.

* **Cycle:** It takes Saturn around two and a half years to transit each sign, and around twenty-nine years to cover the whole zodiac.

URANUS

Mutation. This planet's task is to awaken consciousness through surprises that lead you to originality. Uranus alters your plans and pushes you to improvise. It is everything that is not written, what is eternally new and inexplicable. Represented by electricity, Uranus is change. The sign where your Uranus is placed represents the way you came to deprogram yourself.

* **Verbs:** Free, change, revolutionize.

If your Uranus is in Sagittarius, expansive connections are part of your essential paradigm.

* **Cycle:** Uranus spends seven years in each sign, and it takes around eighty-four years to cover the whole zodiac.

NEPTUNE

Sensitivity. Neptune's task is to dissolve and hydrate the boundaries of your ego, so that you can resonate with wider realities. It reminds you that we are all made of stardust, regardless of apparent differences. Neptune connects you to inspiration and silence. The sign where Neptune is placed offers a hint on how you will lower your guard and let life flow.

* **Verbs:** Dissolve, empathize, open.

If you were born with Neptune in Capricorn, as are many entrepreneurs dedicated to spiritual topics, you came to Earth to transcend the boundaries of what is "real."

* **Cycle:** Neptune spends thirteen and a half years in each sign, and it takes around 165 years to cover the whole zodiac.

PLUTO

Purification. This is the darkest and most magnetic planet. Its strength allows you to release pain, but it demands something in exchange: you need to come face to face with what you fear most and destroy it. Pluto's action cleanses what is stagnant so it becomes a creative force. The sign where Pluto is placed illuminates how you become empowered.

* **Verbs:** Transmute, destroy, eliminate.

If you were born with Pluto in Scorpio, you realize that true power lies in being aware of your own vulnerability.

* **Cycle:** Pluto spends between twelve and eighteen years in each sign, and it takes around 250 years to cover the whole zodiac. Its trajectory is irregular.

CHIRON

Healing. Chiron represents the wound you were born with. But, as with any scar, that's where light enters. Healing cannot be selfish; it must be selfless. The sign where your Chiron is placed indicates the area where you feel hurt, but it's also where you are called to grow by helping others who share that wound.

* **Verbs:** Treat, heal, scar.

If you were born with Chiron in Cancer, your wound is related to the maternal bond.

* **Cycle:** Chiron spends between one and a half to eight years in each sign, and it takes fifty-one years to cover the whole zodiac. Its trajectory is irregular.

NODES

The nodes are mathematical points determined by the Moon's orbit around the Earth. The information they offer is subtle and subconscious. The nodes point toward an evolutive direction that is necessary to take to move to a higher level. The North Node points in the direction of your evolution, while the South Node represents the kind of energy you need to let go of. For example, if your North Node is in Aries, you should learn to follow your desire. If your South Node is in Libra, you must let go of the need for other people's approval. Both points refer to a relationship to integrate. The North Node and South Node are complementary. If you can reach the alchemy between both, you'll realize that the further you go in one direction (north), the further you retreat—on another level of consciousness—to the starting point (south).

PLANETARY CYCLES

Retrogradation is the part of the cycle during which a planet seems to move backward, from the Earth's point of view. This is an apparent movement, not real. It happens when the Earth's orbit reaches and overtakes another planet's orbit. A retrograde planet is revising its function. This process generates inhibition in the external world, inviting you to introspection. The purpose is to become more conscious of lessons learned.

THE FAMOUS MERCURY RETROGRADE

Mercury goes retrograde for three weeks, three times a year. That's a lot! Is that why it is so popular?

To understand the consequences of this movement, which can't be standardized, it's important to observe the sign in which the process takes place. Mercury retrograde enhances awareness of your communication skills and thoughts and the focus of your attention. For the mind to self-examine, it is important to set distractions aside: your cellphone breaks, your internet connection is down, flights get canceled. You may take each misfortune as a sign that it's time to be available for the present moment.

For example, with Mercury retrograde in Pisces, secrets arise from the bottom of the ocean. This connects you to inspiration, intuition, and sensitivity.

SATURN RETURN

Every twenty-nine and a half years, Saturn returns to the natal position. This means that before the ages of thirty, sixty, and ninety, we experience one of Saturn's returns. The first return is probably the most shocking one, as well as the most well known, marking a transition in your passage to adulthood.

Saturn represents the part of your character that acts as authority. Although many people try to ignore it, this return is a powerful event. Saturn asks you to build based on your essential nature. Letting others control your life means losing it.

Saturn's return enables you to integrate your Moon, those markers of childhood you are still attached to. Letting your Moon mature means leaving behind a defensive attitude in order to widen your emotional consciousness. This process sheds light on your wounds, allowing you to heal them.

THE TWELVE MOONS

Here are the attributes for people when the Moon is in each sign of a natal chart.

MOON IN ARIES

Independence makes them feel safe. Therefore, they find it hard to negotiate with others. They take risks based on emotion and attack to defend themselves. What happens if they stop and feel?

MOON IN TAURUS

They find it hard to go through the turbulence that comes with transformation. They mistake possession for affection. Life teaches them to trust and be open.

MOON IN GEMINI

There is no security without explanation, words, or thoughts. They are afraid to choose, but life teaches them to make commitments in order to grow.

MOON IN CANCER

An extreme level of susceptibility prevents them from taking themselves seriously. Life pushes them to fly away from the protection of others.

MOON IN LEO

Being cared for is not the same as having fans. They gain freedom when they don't take everything personally. They need to learn not to care about being important.

MOON IN VIRGO

They obsess about details while the world falls down around them. They fear chaos, which is why life leads them from a closed circle to an expansive spiral.

MOON IN LIBRA

Fear of disputes makes them agree with whatever they are being told. They avoid letting others down. They feel more confident in pairs. They need to leave diplomacy behind in order to grow.

MOON IN SCORPIO

They have a talent to sense when something is fishy. They play emotional power games. Although they fear surrendering themselves, they are called to live love without suffering.

MOON IN SAGITTARIUS

They exaggerate to convince themselves, which may lead them to denial. The lesson for them is that things are not always perfect. Understanding this can be of great value.

MOON IN CAPRICORN

For them, emotions are a sign of dependence, that's why they fear looking vulnerable. They must dare to be soft.

MOON IN AQUARIUS

To achieve significant goals or experience true freedom, they must actively engage and commit to something and not just passively wish for it.

MOON IN PISCES

Reality seems too brutal for them, and they find it hard to set boundaries. Being afraid of separation, they tend to symbiosis. At first, they are disillusioned, then they conquer their dreams.

THE LUNAR CYCLE

There is no place where we can stay forever. The Moon brings about the challenge of detachment. It influences our biological and emotional rhythms. The lunar cycle lasts twenty-nine and a half days. That is the time it takes the Moon to move around the whole zodiac. Compared to the Sun, which makes a complete cycle around the zodiac in a year, the Moon has a fast cycle. The Moon spends two to three days in each sign.

NEW MOON

The Moon is now invisible to us, as it's placed exactly between the Earth and the Sun. We are starting a new cycle. The energy is too low to act, but there is enough to sow intentions to develop new ways, habits, and purposes.

FULL MOON

The Moon is now a glowing mirror reflecting the sunlight. During this phase, we see the fruit of what we've started. Our power and intuition increase. We even dream more than usual. This phase symbolizes culmination.

WAXING MOON

The Moon is now placed at a right angle to the Earth and the Sun, so it is becoming visible. The lunar energy grows, and we become stronger and are able let our intentions grow. We assimilate and nurture more easily. It's a receptive moment.

WANING MOON

We see the Moon getting smaller as the cycle begins its final phase. It's time for conclusions. We lose energy and want to rest. Silencing your mind is a way of collaborating with this process. We let go until the next new Moon.

DRAW YOUR OWN NATAL CHART

***I was born on*____________ *at*______ *in*__________________________**

- Go to *www.astro.com*. Click the "My Astro" link in the upper right corner.
- Enter your details to sign up for free or use the guest access.
- Enter your birth details: date, exact time, and place.
- Choose "Extended Chart Selection."

Hocus-pocus! There you are—your natal chart right in front of your eyes. Copy it on the following page.

- First, draw the internal parts of the mandala. They are the houses. You can add a number inside each to find them easily.
- Identify your ascendant—the sign of the first house—and complete the rest of the wheel by adding the zodiac signs in order in the following houses. You can make each sign a different color. Make sure the midheaven sign (MC) is at the top.
- Find your Sun and Moon. What degrees are they on? The number next to each star is the degree.
- Do the same with each of the planets: Mercury, Venus, Mars, and so on. Use the degrees as reference.
- Find your North Node and place it on the chart, paying attention to its exact position.

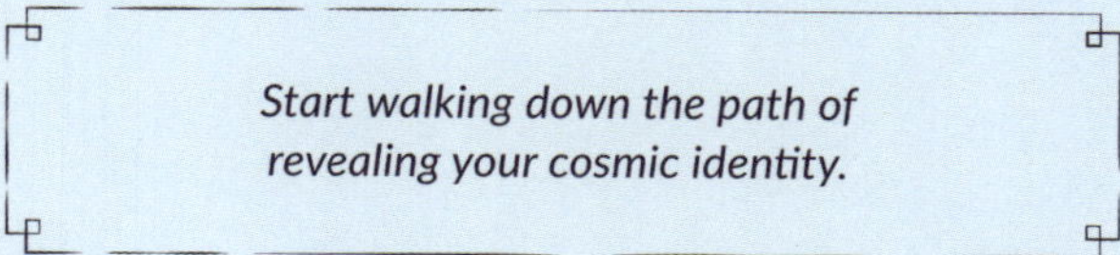

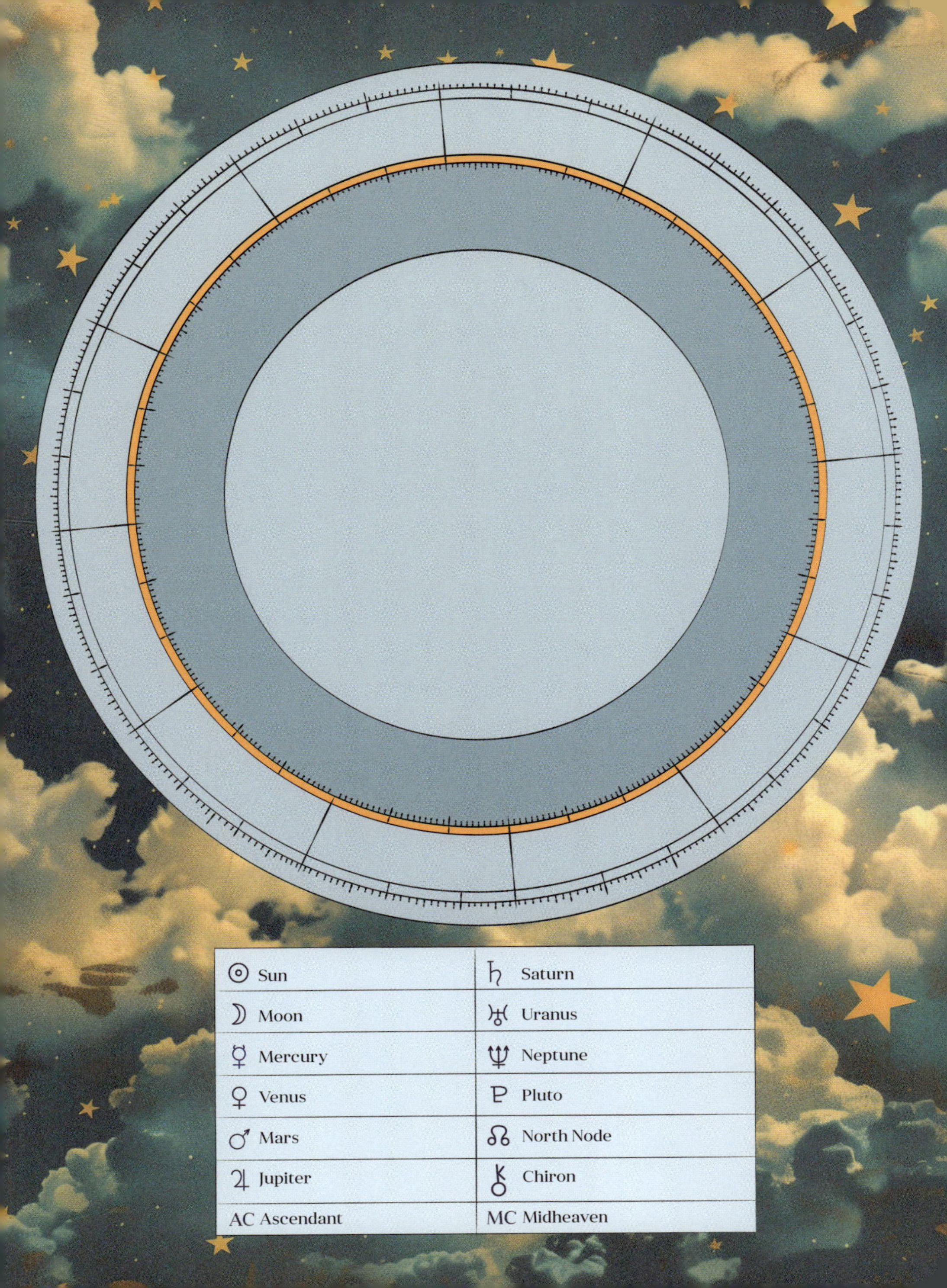

☉ Sun
♄ Saturn
☽ Moon
♅ Uranus
☿ Mercury
♆ Neptune
♀ Venus
♇ Pluto
♂ Mars
☊ North Node
♃ Jupiter
⚷ Chiron
AC Ascendant
MC Midheaven

BALANCE OF ELEMENTS

Let's see what you are made of!

- Check the element of the sign where your Sun is. Do the same with the Moon. Draw them in the diagram. Use the chart below as a reference.
- Do the same with Mercury, Venus, Mars, Jupiter, and Saturn. What signs do your planets have? Identify the elements they belong to and place them in the corresponding quadrants.
- Use the chart to verify what planet rules your rising sign. For example, if your chart shows Taurus rising, it's ruled by Venus. Now take a look at the sign where Venus is in your chart. What element does it belong to? Place it in the diagram as the ascendant ruler (AC R).
- Add up the numbers in each quadrant for a total of ten. Each planet and the ascendant are worth one point, but the Sun and the Moon are worth two points.
- Now convert the number of points in each quadrant to a percentage. For example, if Fire has the Moon (two points), the Sun (two points), and Mercury (one point), that will add up to five points for this quadrant: 0.5 = 50%. It means you are 50 percent Fire.

What percentage of elements do you have in your natal chart?
Look up their meanings on page 18.

SIGN	RULING PLANET	ELEMENT
♈ Aries	♂ Mars	
♌ Leo	☉ Sun	
♐ Sagittarius	♃ Jupiter	Fire
♉ Taurus	♀ Venus	
♍ Virgo	☿ Mercury	
♑ Capricorn	♄ Saturn	Earth
♊ Gemini	☿ Mercury	
♎ Libra	♀ Venus	
♒ Aquarius	♅ Uranus	Air
♋ Cancer	☽ Moon	
♏ Scorpio	♇ Pluto	
♓ Pisces	♆ Neptune	Water

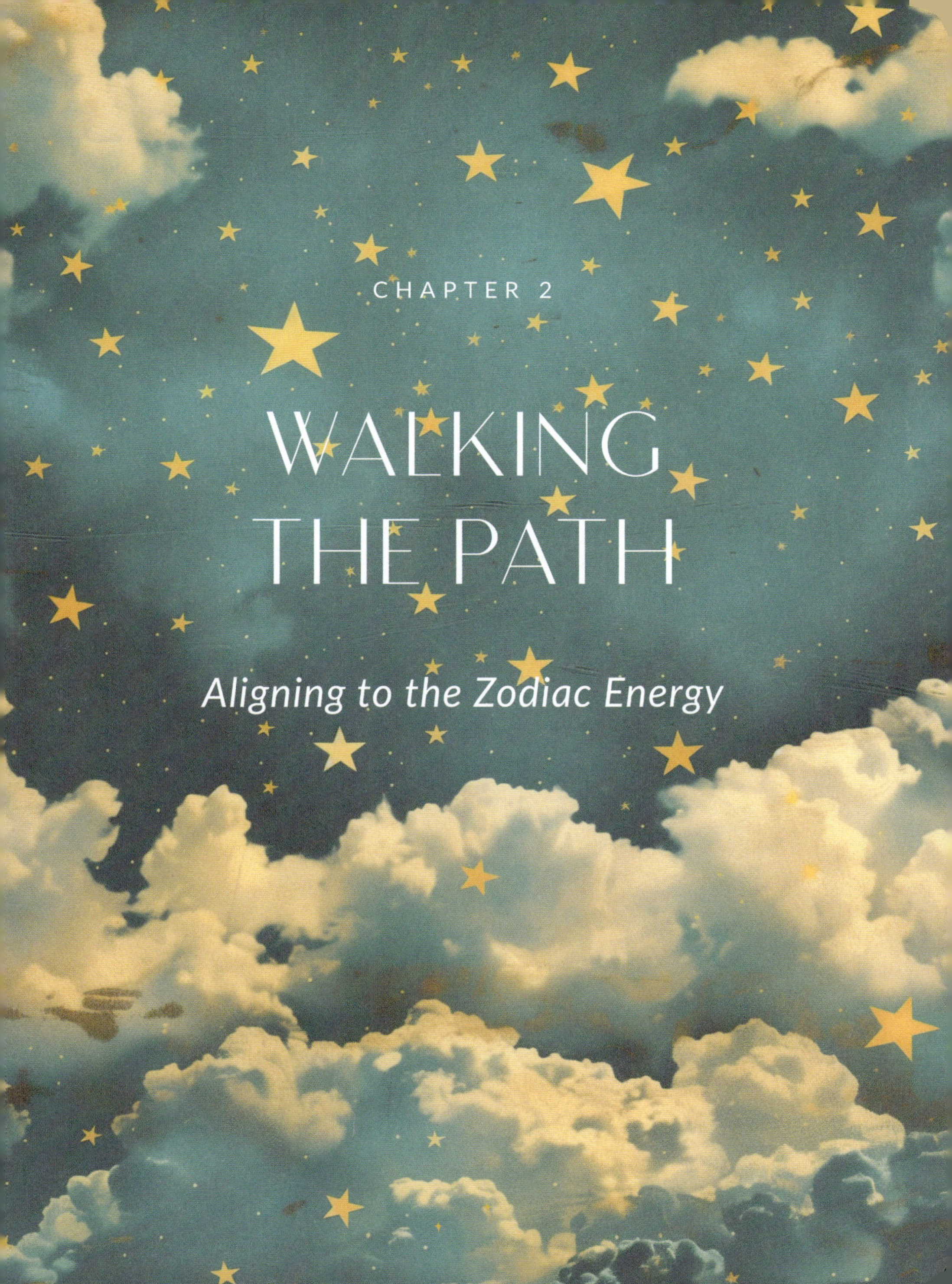

CHAPTER 2

WALKING THE PATH

Aligning to the Zodiac Energy

CHAPTER 2

I am worth the risks I take.

MARCH 21 - APRIL 20

Element: Fire starter

DESIRE - IMPULSE - INSTINCT

ARIES PROFILE

Ruling planet:
Mars, god of war

Complementary opposite:
Libra, the energy of balance and harmony

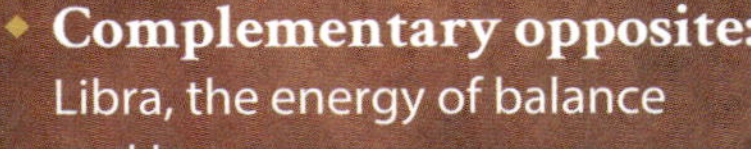

Aligned:
Assertiveness, determination

Off axis:
Anger, aggressiveness

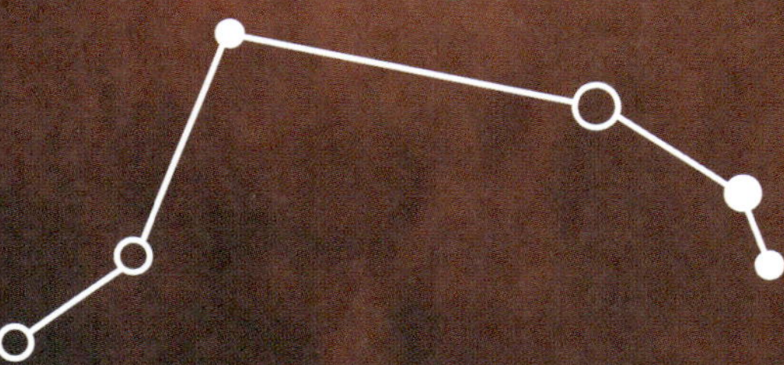

Aries muse:

Emma Watson, April 15, 1990

Emma's determination was first on display at age eleven when she went for the part of Hermione Granger in the Harry Potter movies. After those movies, she successfully continued her career as an adult actress. She also actively advocates for women's and gender equality rights and has been appointed a UN Women goodwill ambassador.

STARTING

PLANTING THE SEED

INVOKE THE ENERGY

I connect with desire as a driving force. My instinct guides me. I am what I do, the energy that drives life. My strength is within. My mission is to act. To take the first breath. To open my eyes and wake up. To sow the idea. My desire is always new and breaks through the doors of existence. Stars explode into being. That's how I move forward.

Through my actions, I decide to be in awareness. For every seed I plant, a door opens. Turning my aggressiveness into power makes me assertive.

PHASE 1

Identify your desire. Motivation. Enthusiastically wish for a lot. This is the time for a storm of "I want." Here I get going and break through.

PURPOSE

- What do you want to start?
- Where is your desire?
- What new seeds will you sow that will bear fruit along the way?

ARIES

1) Identifying your desires: A wish list

Make a quick list of your wishes. They can be distant, impossible, or completely possible. Impulse is all that matters: this is your moment to wish with abandon.

★ **Read them out loud.** Cross out those wishes that are more like obligations.

★ **Eliminate those that imply helping others.** For example: "I want my mother to be happy."

★ **Cross out those wishes that you have already fulfilled** or that are part of your routine. That is, something you might like to do again, but it's not something new; or you like doing it, but you do it every day.

★ **Cross out those wishes that remind you of something familiar**. For example, "I want to return to the town where . . ."

★ **Cross out those wishes that refer only to material things**, like "get a new car."

★ Are any of the wishes expressed in the negative? **Turn them into positive messages.** For example, change "have no more crises" to "live peacefully."

★ **It's time to add wishes**. Is there any wish you have not added to the list because you felt embarrassed or thought it was too late to wish for it?

★ If you wished for something like "world peace," ask yourself **how you could make that something that is closer to you**. Maybe what you want is peace of mind.

There you go! What wishes remain on your list?

Write them down on separate pieces of paper and do a ritual draw. The one you randomly pick is the one you can start acting on. Your subconscious is telling you to go that way.

Write it down here:

Note: This exercise is intended to help you discover your purpose. When in doubt, stay with the concrete desires that have to do with *you*.

ARIES

2) Activation exercise: Awakening your inner fire

- **No matter where you are or what you are wearing, go outside.** Your goal is to run two blocks, take a walk, or do anything that gets your body moving. If your body asks you for more, just follow your impulse. Don't forget to return to this journal.

- **On a piece of paper, write down everything that caught your attention.** What were your thoughts?

CONCERNS	INSPIRATIONS

- Whatever comes to your mind now is related to your purpose.
  How can you connect to that?

Let's wipe away worries with the ritual on the following page!

In case of excess Aries energy, integrate Libra energy:

- **Call someone you want to get together with.** Let them choose everything: where to go, what to eat, what to do, what music to listen to. The challenge is to let somebody else call the shots. Just propose the meeting. Record what happens.

ARIES RITUAL

CLEANSING THE ENEMIES OF DESIRE

Anger, shame, and doubt can work as obstacles to your desires. Anger is a fuel that invites you to act. You can reverse the energy charge to activate your purpose with this ritual.

1. **Wear comfortable clothes.** Choose a big room and move furniture out of the away. Find an African percussion playlist and play it at top volume.

2. **Dance!** Let your body flow. Jump, squat, stand up again. Anger, shame, and obstacles are sweated away. Each drop of sweat removes pent-up frustrations from your body. Don't stop. The idea is to let it all go; it's even okay to shout and cry. Dance as you please.

Congratulations, you are actively meditating!

3. Panting heavily and with a sweaty forehead, **grab a pen and rewrite your desires**. Don't look at the previous page! Just follow your impulse.

Life is short. Don't be lazy.

APRIL 20 - MAY 21

Element: Earth as prime matter

GENERATING - CONSERVING - ENJOYING

TAURUS PROFILE

- **Ruling planet:** Venus, goddess of love
- **Complementary opposite:** Scorpio, representing the need for transformation
- **Aligned:** Self-worth, sensuality
- **Off axis:** Accumulation, laziness

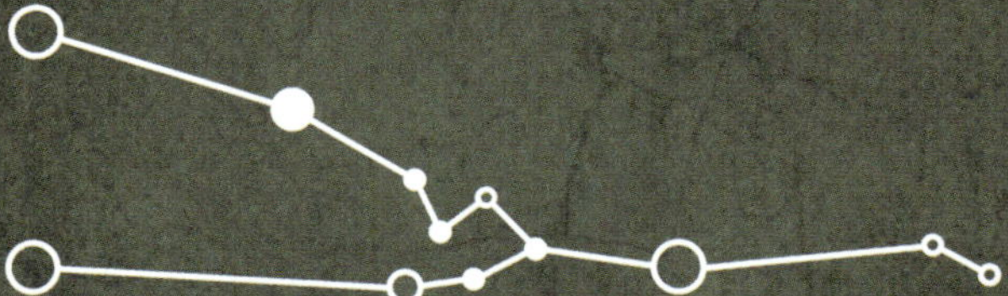

- **Taurus muse:**

Sophia Amoruso, April 20, 1984

She was the creator of a clothing store called Nasty Girl, which started on eBay. A natural-born Girl Boss, Sophia delivered orders to all corners of the United States from her bedroom. Sophia is one of the cusp women in this book, having been born on a transitional date between the signs of Taurus and Aries. Have you noticed she shares her birthday with the Aries muse? Both her natal chart and everything we know about Sophia tells us she is a Taurus, but her driving force is undeniably Aries.

To learn more about cusps, go to page 21.

MATERIALIZING

TURNING THE SEED INTO SUBSTANCE

INVOKE THE ENERGY

Fertile soil is an extension of the heavens. My body calls me to feed my impulses. I slow down. Stillness helps me rest. My veins are roots delving into matter. I gather from the soil the necessary nutrients, and I root to grow.

Life grants me countless material and spiritual resources. My strength lies in the ability to multiply them. I trust the generous power of nature. I sustain love in my processes. I value and enjoy life, simply and naturally.

PHASE 2

A moment to materialize, checking out if the desire is solid and necessary. Evaluate your income and available resources. They may be inner or outer resources, subtle or concrete. It's time to inhabit your body, generate stability, and cover your needs.

PURPOSE

- What will you materialize?
- What resources do you have to do this?
- What energy will you invest in it?

TAURUS

1) Materializing: Feeding your purpose

Use this journal to define what needs arise from your wish.

★ **What do you need to materialize?** Resources, money, time, logistics.

★ **What is your situation in terms of time?** How are you handling it?

★ **Where will you find the resources that you need to start?**

★ **What are your beliefs as regards the material realm?** Write down at least three.

It is possible that at this moment you feel inertia because of things that will need to be done. If you are feeling discouraged, you can go straight to this phase's ritual.

TAURUS

2) Activation exercise: Rooting

- **Take a walk in a nearby park.** Take off your shoes and let your feet touch the ground. What does it feel like?

- **Now choose a tree and hug it.** Yes. Give it a tight hug! Stay there for at least two minutes. Can you feel its anchor? A tree is, first of all, firm. It is not afraid to stay right where it is. Every time you want to embrace your purpose, try the tree-hugging practice. It is also useful whenever you are feeling unmotivated or your energy is low.

- **Write, draw, or record your experience of the physical sensations of this exercise.**

In case of excess Taurus energy, integrate Scorpio energy:

- **Give away five items of clothing that you no longer wear but are in good condition.** Wash and gift wrap each of them. Give this offering to a special person.

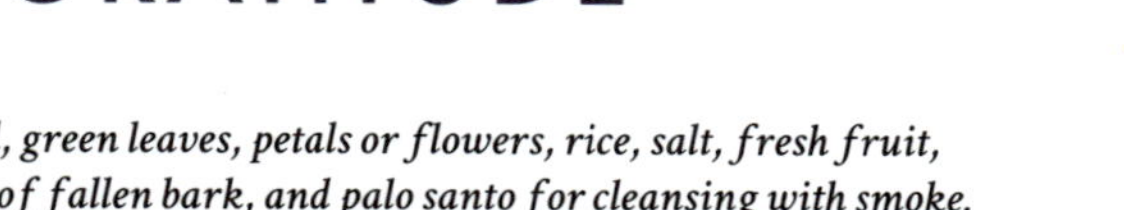

TAURUS RITUAL

GRATITUDE

You will need: soil, green leaves, petals or flowers, rice, salt, fresh fruit, seeds, coins, a piece of fallen bark, and palo santo for cleansing with smoke. (Note: be sure to obtain your materials from sustainable sources.)

1. Place the ritual items in a circle and light the palo santo so that you fill the room with its aroma. Let yourself soak in the smoke. Now put your hands together and pay attention to all these objects. Thank them for helping you get closer to your purpose.

2. Who do you thank for these experiences? What was required to realize them? Think of both inner and outer resources.

3. Let the answer grant you awareness: value everything that you materialize in life.

The art of thinking risk-free

MAY 21 - JUNE 21

Element: Mental air

PLAYFUL - COMMUNICATIVE - CONNECTING

GEMINI PROFILE

- **Ruling planet:** Mercury, the messenger of the heavens
- **Complementary opposite:** Sagittarius, directing and orienting your search
- **Aligned:** Diversity, communication
- **Off axis:** Fragmentation, doubt

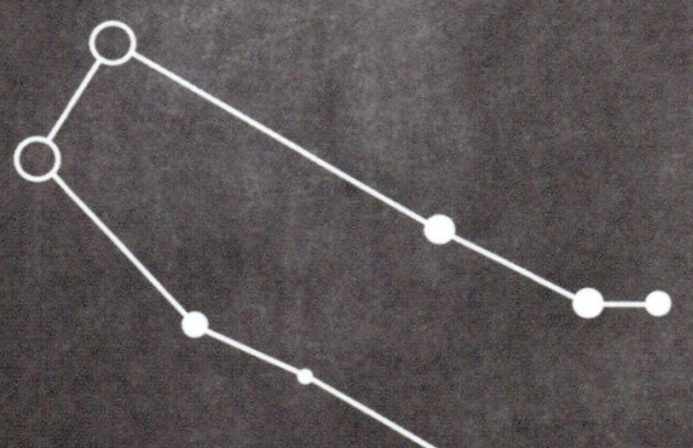

- **Gemini muse:**

Vanessa Bell, May 28, 1879

A bohemian painter and interior designer, she was part of the Bloomsbury Group. She was Virginia Woolf's sister and was very close to her. A shared passion for art and beauty made their bond stronger.

CONNECTING

LETTING INNER PARTS COMMUNICATE

INVOKE THE ENERGY

My curiosity paves the way. I perceive the universe in terms of relationships. I am mind, thought, and voice. I choose the right words to communicate. When the heart speaks, even a deaf person can hear. My words are powerful and promise to transform. An infinite network connects diversity.

My beginner's mind is fresh and open. There are questions I cannot answer. I'm not afraid to experiment and learn or to try to grow. I accept my contradictions and doubts so that my truth emerges. Choosing makes me strong. I am a bridge. Communication is my gift.

PHASE 3

Unfolding options, seeing all the possible ways of achieving what you want with what you have. Brainstorming. This is an experimental phase to try new ways of doing things.

PURPOSE

- How many possible ways are there to keep moving?
- What are you communicating?
- How can you connect your inner thoughts with the material world?

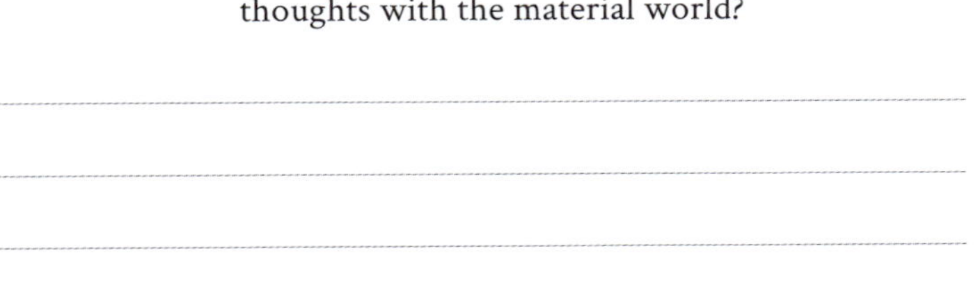

GEMINI

1) Communicating: Unfolding options

Once you know the resources you can count on to get what you want, it's time to look at the range of options.

★ **If you had to explain this process to somebody, what would you say?**

★ **Do some brainstorming on options for moving forward.** Then call that person and tell them about your purpose. You can include doubts, other people involved, spontaneous thoughts, requisites, and contradictions.

★ **What insight does it grant you?** Write that point of view here:

2) Activation exercise: The keyword

- **Take a new route to some of the places you usually visit. Choose a stranger along the way.** Follow them for as long as you can (without being creepy) and adopt their energy. Try to see the world through their eyes. What word comes to mind?

Write that keyword down here: ....

- **Begin a free association writing exercise starting with that keyword.** For example, if the word is "stress," the chain could be: "Work, tiredness, pillow, holidays, ice cream, cold, igloo, Christmas."

- **How many of those words are connected to your process?** How do they reinforce your message? If you'd like, choose another word and free associate again to help you connect to your purpose.

In case of excess Gemini energy, integrate Sagittarius energy:

- **Spend a whole day in silence. If you can, try not to talk at all.** Communicate in other ways. Or, try spending a whole day without going on social media. You choose! Did this exercise change your perspective? Did it help you better connect to your purpose?

GEMINI RITUAL

FIGHTING HESITATION

You will need: incense, a quiet place, paper, and a pencil

Exploring multiple possibilities can be stressful. It's normal to feel like you're going in circles only to end up where you started. This ritual will help you through the process.

1. Light an incense stick, close your eyes, and picture a bird flying in the open sky. Imagine its movements and how it soars in flight. Observe the size of its wings, the colors, and the landscape around it.

2. Ask the bird to guide you. Complete the following intentions:

I need a favoring wind for: ____________________

May the wind take away: ____________________

I will clear my mind with: ____________________

I need a break from: ____________________

3. Write the keywords for these intentions on a piece of paper, then make a paper airplane from it. Launch it from a window and let it fly.

4. To finish the ritual, say these words:

I can fly free

He who looks inside, grows.

JUNE 21 - JULY 22

Element: Water of the first emotions

INTIMACY - IMAGINATION - SENSITIVITY

CANCER PROFILE

- **Ruling planet:**
The Moon, protector of emotions and enabler of contact

- **Complementary opposite:**
Capricorn, encouraging going out into the world

- **Aligned:**
Emotional security, a sense of belonging

- **Off axis:**
Dependence, immaturity

- **Cancer muse:**

Diana, Princess of Wales, July 1, 1961

The most vulnerable princess we've seen. She let her heart guide her and transcended the cliché of a fairy-tale princess. She represented motherhood far beyond her home, and her social work will be remembered in history.

CONTAINING

MAKING A FOUNDATION

INVOKE THE ENERGY

I go inward looking for intimacy. I connect to emotion and contact my vulnerability. Inhabiting myself is being present. My body is my temple, my home. I belong where I give my time. My strength is my warmth. My emotions are intelligent and allow me to discern.

My roots come from the past and nurture the present. I receive messages from my ancestors who hold me in a tender embrace and guide my emotional leadership. I experience self-transcendence by honoring my childhood.

PHASE 4

Choose what you will give your time to. It is time to close and leave behind what no longer serves you. Choose to align with what you identify with the most. Here and now, start defining where you are going. Inner world.

PURPOSE

- What do you decide to take care of for the process to move on?
- What do you leave behind because it does not represent you anymore?
- What do you want to grow and become stronger?

CANCER

1) Supporting: Swimming in my own universe

INSIDE

★ **What feelings are triggered by your purpose?** Inspirations you get:

OUTSIDE

★ **What is your life like now?** Signs you receive from others:

★ **Match each statement with a symbolic image.** For example: "Internally, I feel excited" → stars

★ **To unify yourself,** create your own message by linking the inner images with the outer ones.

CANCER

2) Activation exercise: Remembering and connecting

- **Record a log of your journey from childhood to the present, listing all the milestones of your life. Choose a title for each stage.**

- **Now do the same with your purpose, from when it started until today. If you prefer, this record can be digital. Create a folder on your computer with many inspirational images that help you connect to the story of this process.**

Don't forget to leave a record of it here!

In case of excess Cancer energy, integrate Capricorn energy:

- **Go to a party or event where you don't know anyone. Talk to someone new.** The idea is not to mention your past during the conversation. If you want to double the stakes, invent a new name for yourself and tell something fictional about yourself. Be somebody else.

What I take from this conversation is:

CANCER RITUAL

RELEASE

You will need: paper and pencil, a bowl with purified water, a white candle, a ball of yarn, a pair of scissors.

1. Light a white candle and place it next to a bowl full of water.

2. Write down all the memories you want to forget. They may be words that had an impact on you, negative thoughts, or wounds you carry with you. Write down the names of the people involved, as well as the dates when these things took place. Be thorough. Even if it hurts, it's necessary.

3. Take the ball of yarn and tie a knot for every thought, person, or memory. Follow your instincts to decide the distance between each knot. Take your time. When you feel you're done, tie one extra knot.

4. Start your releasing ritual. Take the scissors and cut the yarn. Make a cut for every knot and hold a thought of light. Feel yourself cutting those ties that kept you faithful to an old narrative, preventing you from connecting with your purpose.

5. When you're done, throw away the pieces of yarn and take the trash out immediately.

LEO

The greatest victory is being able to live with yourself.

JULY 23 - AUGUST 22

Element: Fire of the heart

AUTHENTICITY - DIGNITY - SELF-EXPRESSION

LEO PROFILE

- **Ruling planet:** The Sun, source of energy and vitality

- **Complementary opposite:** Aquarius, energy that leads you to offer your difference to the group

- **Aligned:** Love, generosity

- **Off axis:** Self-centeredness, arrogance

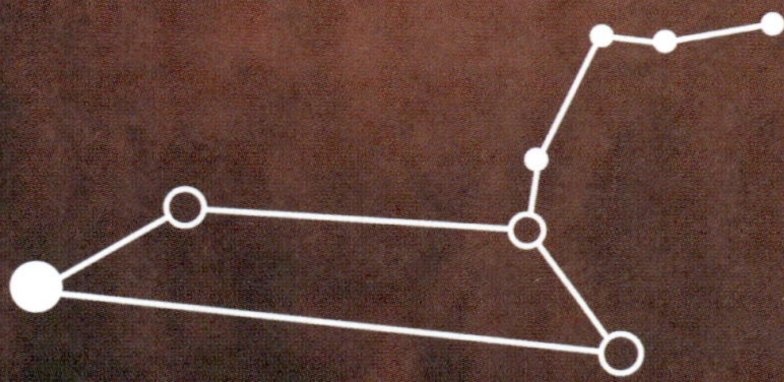

- **Leo muse:**

Jennifer Lynn Lopez, July 24, 1969

J Lo is an American icon. As a singer, dancer, actress, and entrepreneur, she has inspired many people with her glow. She has also challenged beauty standards, as an authentic Leo would. Jennifer champions noble causes such as peace, equal rights, and the LGBTQIA+ community.

CREATING

VISIBLE SELF-EXPRESSION

INVOKE THE ENERGY

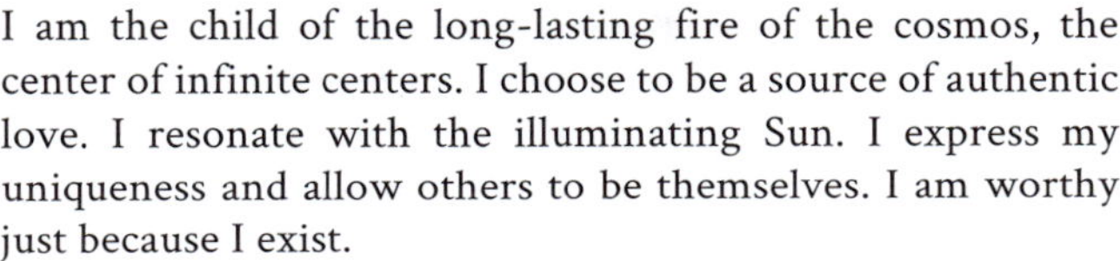

I am the child of the long-lasting fire of the cosmos, the center of infinite centers. I choose to be a source of authentic love. I resonate with the illuminating Sun. I express my uniqueness and allow others to be themselves. I am worthy just because I exist.

I free my presence by embracing my insecurity. I was born to manifest the strength I was given. I discover my world and surrender to it with all my heart. I learn it's not darkness that scares me but my own light.

PHASE 5

Be yourself. Time to express what was brewing inside. Find your own identity; give it a name. It's a time of authorship that requires creativity and singularity. The challenge is to move from the search for acknowledgment to self-love.

PURPOSE

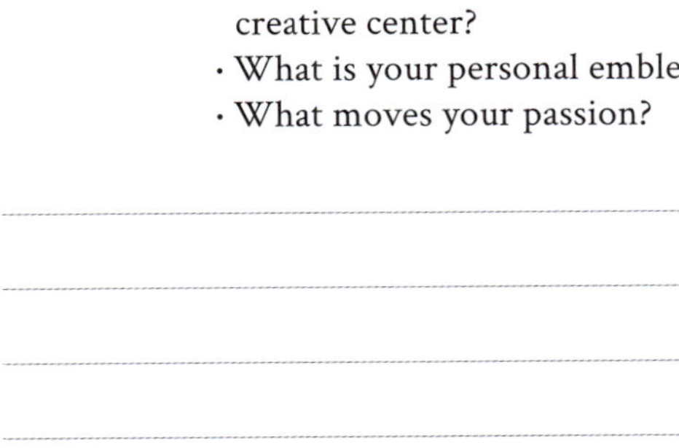

- What will you express from your creative center?
- What is your personal emblem?
- What moves your passion?

LEO

1) Creating: Expressing is naming

Give a name to your purpose. This will allow you to give it its own identity and let it shine for itself. The following questions will help you come up with a name by thinking of some identifying qualities.

What color is your purpose?	What animal might represent it?	What artist could cocreate with it?
What kind of music and sound surround it?	Think of a lucky charm to give it strength.	What is its motto?

MY PURPOSE'S NAME IS:

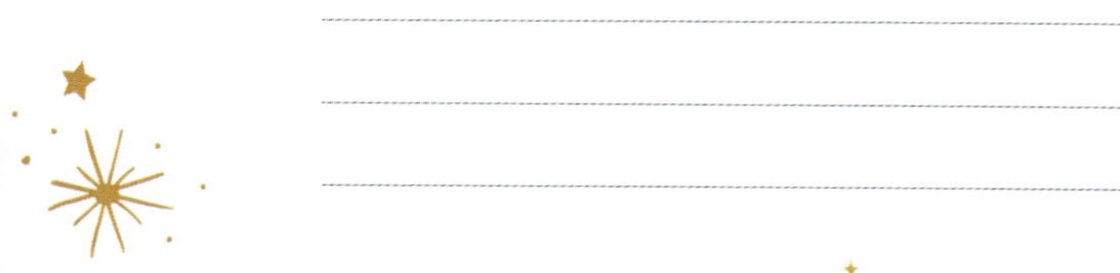

2) Activation exercise: Self-perception

- **Draw your self-portrait. Have you ever tried?** Do it without lifting the pencil from the paper and without looking at the page even once—just look at yourself in the mirror. Make two versions. Paint each one with different colors and backgrounds.

- **Now that you have freed yourself, do you dare design the logo and motto of your purpose?** Based on its name, and using the elements you used to find it, think of a logo. You don't need to know how to draw. You can collage or improvise some lettering.

In case of excess Leo energy, integrate Aquarius energy:

- **For one week, use somebody else's photo as your profile picture on social media.** What do you admire in that person that you can adopt as an attitude in this moment of expression?

LEO RITUAL

HEARTBEAT

You will need: a sunrise.

1. Sit down with you legs folded and a straight back, facing the sun. Be aware of your connection to it. Inhale, exhale, and close your eyes. Consciously breathe in and out five more times.

2. Now place your hand over your heart. Feel your heartbeat. Inhale and exhale five more times, noticing how your heartbeat matches your breathing

3. Identify your pulse and feel how the rising sun rekindles your inner flame. When the sun is well above the horizon, give thanks and go about your day.

There's a place for everyone, even in chaos.

AUGUST 23 - SEPTEMBER 22

Element: Earth with added value

ORDER - SYSTEM - SERVICE

VIRGO PROFILE

- **Ruling planet:** Mercury, the messenger of heaven

- **Complementary opposite:** Pisces, leading to dissolution and flexibility

- **Aligned:** Dedication, humbleness

- **Off axis:** Overthinking, destructive criticism

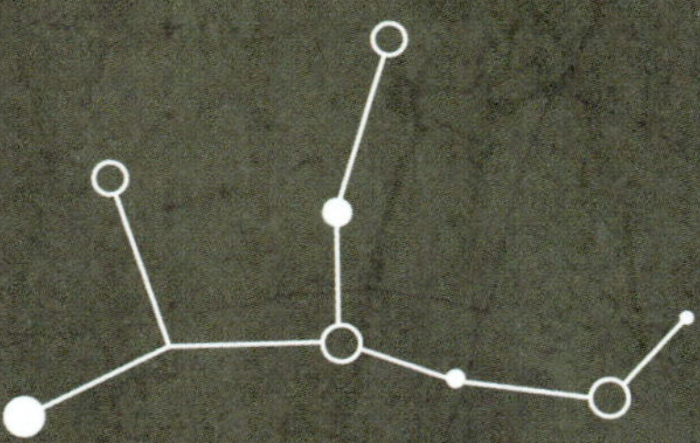

- **Virgo muse:**

Beyoncé Knowles, September 4, 1981

Known as "Queen Bey," Beyoncé is a hard-working singer/songwriter, actress, producer, and businesswoman. She is passionate about each step in any production process, refining every detail in order to give her fans the "perfect" experience. As a true Virgo, she values her private life and tries to keep her focus off the cameras.

ANALYZING

ADJUSTING THE PARTS

INVOKE THE ENERGY

There's natural order in the cosmos. I am a crucial part of its mechanism. The universe organizes my tasks, and I accept and respect the steps. I throw away what is not useful to the flow of things. The challenge is to see the patterns without over-adapting to anything.

The process holds secret mysteries. My controlling mind cannot grasp them. I transcend repetition to make my activity sacred. I surrender to the little things because that is where the great things lie. The order I am part of is already perfect. Body, mind, and heart work in tune.

PHASE 6

Optimize the system to improve the overall work. Your task is to perfect what you have realized, choose practical utility, define tasks, organize yourself. Do your task with love. Discriminate the small things. It's time to act on what you thought, decide on what you hesitated about.

PURPOSE

- How useful is what has been done?
- What will you adjust or revise in the process so that it works?
- How are your daily routines working to achieve what you want?

VIRGO

1) Understanding: The state of the situation

★ **System:** Make a chart or a list to help you organize the steps to continue the process of achieving your purpose. It is important to choose concrete, clear, and realizable actions.

Method: You can use a reference system with hierarchies. In front of each concept, use a symbol that indicates the type of task it represents, for example:

◆ *a simple task,* ✳ *an event,* ★ *a priority task, or* ▶▶▶ *a detail*

VIRGO

2) Activation exercise: A connection space

- **Make your own inspirational oasis.** Choose a space for your creative process. Clear the space and give it light. Don't just fill the void. Choose a few things that really invite you to connect.

- **Write a manifesto for your space, like the instruction manual of the place.** For example, "I take off my shoes when I enter my sacred space." "I don't use my cell phone while I'm there."

Keep it neat. A tidy space equals a fresh mind.

In case of excess Virgo energy, integrate the Pisces energy:

- **Don't wear a watch for a whole day. Don't look at your calendar. Cancel an appointment.** Be open to improvisation.

VIRGO RITUAL

ENERGETIC CLEANSING

*You will need: a fire-proof bowl, herbs (like myrrh, rosemary, eucalyptus, bay, cinnamon, lavender, rue, lemon or orange peel), activated charcoal, matches.**

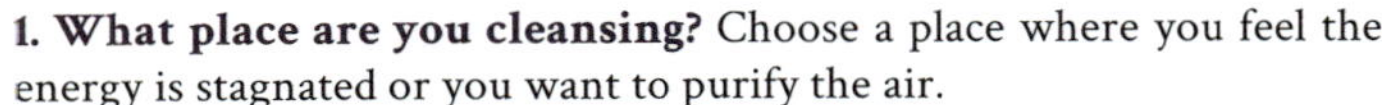

1. What place are you cleansing? Choose a place where you feel the energy is stagnated or you want to purify the air.

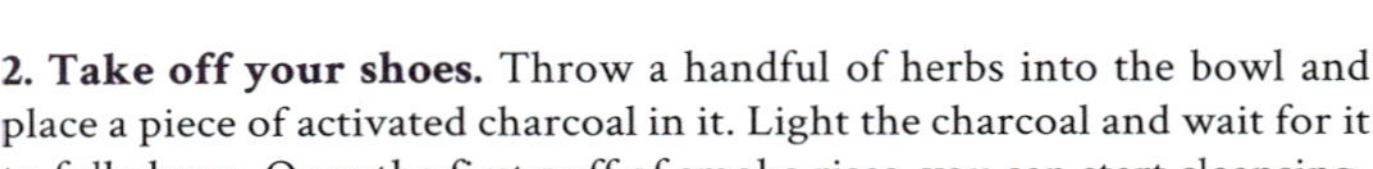

2. Take off your shoes. Throw a handful of herbs into the bowl and place a piece of activated charcoal in it. Light the charcoal and wait for it to fully burn. Once the first puff of smoke rises, you can start cleansing.

3. Move around with this smoke wherever you want to renew the energy. Be careful: the bowl will be hot. Don't grab it with your bare hands. It is important to open the windows so that the area stays ventilated. Make big movements. Don't stay still.

4. When the ashes are cold, spread them outside on fresh soil so the waste turns into nutrition.

---

* *These materials can be found at herbalists' or metaphysical shops.*

LIBRA

Imbalance leads to balance.

SEPTEMBER 23 - OCTOBER 23

Element: Air of harmony

BEAUTY - OPENNESS - JUSTICE

LIBRA PROFILE

- **Ruling planet:** Venus, goddess of love and opening to others

- **Complementary opposite:** Aries, its fire generating the necessary impulse to open to the new

- **Aligned:** Temperance, negotiation

- **Off axis:** Hesitation, being unfaithful to yourself to please others

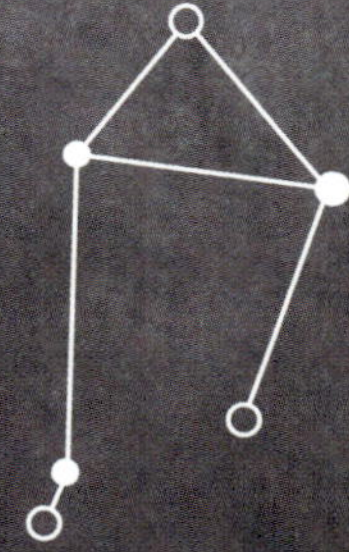

- **Libra muse:**

Gwen Stefani, October 3, 1969

Gwen is a style and music icon. She proudly declares her astrological identity in the song "Spark the Fire." Undoubtedly, the combination of her charisma and hard work has helped her balance the scales with the ups and downs of life.

HARMONIZING

NEW BALANCE

INVOKE THE ENERGY

The right balance harmonizes opposites. Like a great self-regulated ecosystem, day and night attract and cooperate with each other. I open to all this beauty, because how others see me reflects what I don't know about myself. All the universe depends on the relationships between its elements.

My actions are conciliatory, and my gift is to get along well with others. My strength lies in perceiving ephemeral states. Each movement is followed by a response. Sometimes I decide, sometimes I don't. I straddle the line so as to respect the whole.

PHASE 7

Something has been organized and reaches a new balance. It's time to see what you haven't considered yet: repolarization. Knowledge of your shadow comes and you can incorporate it. It appears through your connections with others.

PURPOSE

- What external information is showing your imbalance?
- Who can you associate with to keep growing?
- What are you giving and taking?

LIBRA

1) Harmonizing: balancing

★ **Make a list of the people who support your purpose, and another list of those who apparently don't.**

Next to each name, write a word that summarizes your opinion. Don't filter it. Each relationship can reveal something.

★ **Choose a person from each list and make an identikit for them.**
Here are some details to guide you: age, education, profession, colors they wear, zodiac sign, hobbies, what they carry in their bags, music they listen to, spontaneous reactions they create in you.

★ **Ask yourself who the other person truly is.**
What does this person reflect of yourself? And of your project?

LIBRA

2) Activation exercise: Complementing

★ **Go back to the list of tasks created during phase 6 and check who can complement you for some of the pending tasks.**

I can count on: ______________________________

____

For: ______________________________

____

We agree on: ______________________________

____

Result of the experience: ______________________________

____

In case of excess Libra energy, integrate Aries energy:

For a whole week, refuse any plans you don't want to take part in. Did you make some room in your routine?

LIBRA RITUAL

CONTEMPLATION

You will need: twigs, herbs, colorful flowers or seeds.

1. Choose a mystical place in your house to put these objects. A place where they will be undisturbed, such as a bookshelf, a shelf in your closet, or a special table.

2. Once you have them all together, choose the one that calls to you. Select it without thinking; just follow your intuition and give it your full attention. Stop to contemplate it. Don't look for anything in particular in the object; just focus on it.

3. In that state, write whatever you feel:

SCORPIO

I look for what is below
to raise it.

OCTOBER 22 - NOVEMBER 22

Element: Deep and vital water

INTENSITY - SURRENDERING - FUSION

SCORPIO PROFILE

Ruling planet:
Pluto, god of the underworld

Complementary opposite:
Taurus, the impulse to connect to simple things

Aligned:
Regeneration, healing

Off axis:
Control, toxicity

Scorpio muse:

Lorde, November 7, 1996

Lorde is the type of sensitive, deep, and enigmatic singer/song-writer that we can't help but love. She is capable of turning dark waters into something luminous. She has done several charity singles to help medical causes, such as to find a cure for Batten disease and fund the purchase of neurology monitors.

DEEPENING

DESTROYING TO CREATE

INVOKE THE ENERGY

The dark lady of the night lives within my darkness. Her powerful strength calls me to transform. I wish to escape the fear of living. Ancient secrets dwell in the deep. Sexuality is the path to creative energy. I lose innocence to awaken.

Sensitivity and power integrate like light into shadow. In the beauty of intensity, I hit rock bottom to rise up. I surrender to the purge as a portal to healing. All the shadows in the world cannot put out the light of my intuition.

PHASE 8

Pull up the weeds. It's time to contact the deepest levels of the process, which are presented as conflict. You need to get over the drama. Concentration, power, and passion: the ultimate goal is to empower yourself.

PURPOSE

- What needs to be transformed?
- What do you need to get rid of in order to be powerful?
- And the key: What releases your pain?

SCORPIO

1) Deepening: A record of the shadow

★ **Write down all the obstacles that appear when you try to move on with your project.** Draw a doodle for each of them, representing whatever it makes you feel (intensity, melancholy, gentleness, indifference):

SCORPIO

2) Activation exercise: Catharsis

- **For each of the obstacles that appeared, shout to release the associated burden.**

1. Focus your mind's attention on a specific point in your body where you feel tension.
2. Try to become very aware of all the characteristics of this unease.
3. Relax your throat. Take a deep breath and shout, completely emptying your lungs.
4. Allow yourself to breathe freely three or four times, letting change enter your body.
5. Repeat steps three and four until the tension disappears.
6. Record your feelings in this journal.

In case of excess Scorpio energy, integrate Taurus energy:

- **Do some gardening. Visit a friend and take some cuttings from their plants.** Put the cuttings in a glass of water and watch the roots emerge. The idea is to feel your connection with the Earth.

SCORPIO RITUAL

BURNING

You will need: pen and paper, and an envelope.

1. Write a letter to your shadow, telling it everything you think and feel. Don't withhold anything. What can your shadow teach you? Can you thank it for its lessons?

2. Once you're done, put the letter in an envelope and put it in the freezer. Imagine its energy contracting in the cold and darkness.

3. The following day, burn the letter to release its energy. Scatter the ashes outdoors.

SAGITTARIUS

I am optimistic and strive to move forward in a positive direction.

NOVEMBER 22 - DECEMBER 21

Element: Purposeful fire

TRUST - EXPANSION - IDEALS

SAGITTARIUS PROFILE

- **Ruling planet:** Jupiter, god of abundance

- **Complementary opposite:** Gemini, energy that brings variety and play

- **Aligned:** Surrender, transcendence

- **Off axis:** Idealism, arrogance

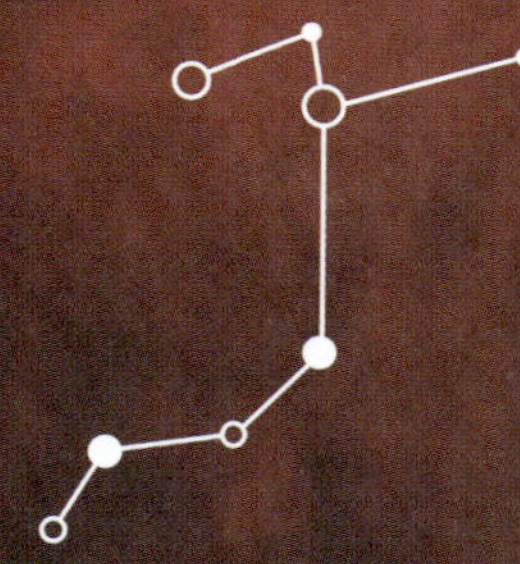

- **Sagittarius muse:**

Taylor Swift, December 13, 1989

Taylor is adventurous, optimistic, and expansive. She is a natural leader who touches the lives of those who let themselves be touched by her lyrics. She is also very generous in sharing her personal experiences and opening her heart to her fans.

UNDERSTANDING

A NEW SYNTHESIS

INVOKE THE ENERGY

I learn from the abundance of life. It is generous with its wisdom and awakens my knowledge. I face adventure with certainty. The path is pure learning. I carry the gift of transmission: at every door I knock upon, I deliver good news.

I understand the mission that was given to me. Wherever I go, I carry truth with me. My guidance is the search for meaning. I am a flowing, self-purifying river. I embrace teaching experiences. I humbly accept living my purpose.

PHASE 9

Time to renew your vows. It is time to integrate what was released during the previous phase and take it to a new level. Meaning is transmitted. It's time to acknowledge the unity that underlies diversity. Don't be afraid to adopt a more comprehensive point of view.

PURPOSE

- How are you going to expand?
- What will you do to grow your purpose?
- What guides you?

1) Understanding: Taking it to another level

★ **Use this pyramid to write the qualities that this process has enhanced in you.** The ones on the base are those that you thought of first. The ones on the top are the most surprising ones.

★ **Inspire yourself:**

During this process, I found that: ....

....

I used to see things in a way that: ....

And now I see things: ....

I got a clear sign that this was the right path when: ....

....

I chose to sacrifice ....

in order to connect to my purpose.

The meaning of all this is related to: ....

....

I keep choosing this project because: ....

SAGITTARIUS

2) Activation exercise: Guiding

- **Draw a map showing the journey you have taken to fulfill your purpose, as if it were a treasure hunt.**

Include on the map the things you have discovered on your way, the bridges you crossed, the paths you took. You may also add those destinations you haven't visited yet.

In case of excess Sagittarius energy, integrate Gemini energy:

- **Invite your friends over for a board game session.** Change one of the main rules of the game.

SAGITTARIUS RITUAL

CHANGING YOUR POINT OF VIEW

You will need: cardboard, markers, and a mat.

1. On a piece of cardboard, write a word that represents your purpose today. Do it in block capital letters. Stick the cardboard on the wall.

2. Sit on the mat at a distance from the cardboard that allows some perspective and do a yoga posture. If you are not used to this, here's a simple one: sit cross-legged with your palms on your knees and look at the ceiling.

3. Without moving your head, shift your focus to the cardboard while you take nine deep breaths.

4. Relax out of the posture and record your new point of view or any ideas that emerged during the practice.

Simplicity is only achieved through hard work.

DECEMBER 22 - JANUARY 20

Element: The steady earth of the mountain

STRUCTURE - RESPONSIBILITY - DISCIPLINE

CAPRICORN PROFILE

Ruling planet:
Saturn, god of time

Complementary opposite:
Cancer, helping you connect to emotional needs

Aligned:
Determination, responsibility

Off axis:
Meanness, severity

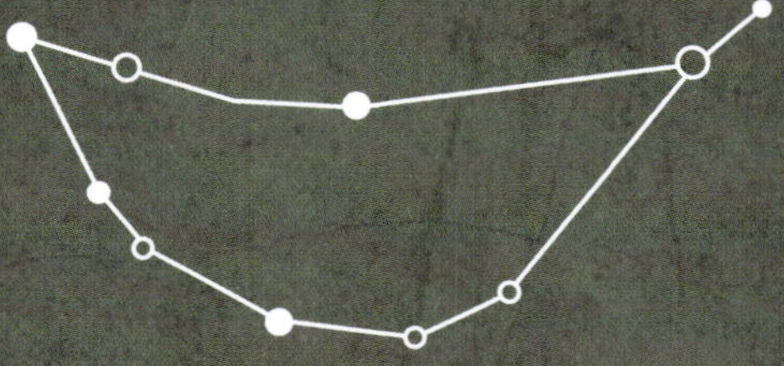

Capricorn muse:

Dolly Parton, January 19, 1946

Singer, songwriter, businesswoman, and philanthropist, Dolly Parton is beloved by multiple generations. Her career is a model of perseverance and hard work. She has said, "The way I see it, if you want the rainbow, you have to put up with the rain." The kindness she shows to others and her joy for life are inspirations.

STRUCTURING

THE RESULT

INVOKE THE ENERGY

I turn everything into matter. My strength lies in the ability to accomplish things. I choose to be my own support and authority. I don't blame anyone nor do I complain, because I choose freely. I consolidate my experience with every step.

There are solid materials at my disposal, and they allow me to build stable worlds. Important things don't happen overnight, and nothing that is real can be threatened. I am part of the supreme law that rules the cosmos. My challenge is to turn boundaries into possibilities.

PHASE 10

Maximum expression of the cycle: final result. Whatever was planted during the Cancer phase now flourishes. The initial impulse is fulfilled. Something definitive has been captured. I commit to my goals and achievements. Fruition, law, projects, and realization.

PURPOSE

- Measure your results and set goals to continue.
- What have you achieved?
- What balance do you gain from this process?

CAPRICORN

1) Structuring: Balance and results

★ **If you are about to do this exercise, it means you have realized your purpose.** This is the moment of "getting on the plane."

Draw a house with a chimney, plus a tree on the lawn.

★ **Use the house as a symbol of your process.** What made up your floor and your roof? What were the advantages? What was the door that opened the way? What does the tree represent to you? And the walls? What is coming out of the chimney?

Now you can invite people over to celebrate!

CAPRICORN

2) Activation exercise: The top

- **Go to the highest point in your city.** Look at the view from there.
- **Open your journal and write down everything you achieved based on your purpose.** Leave a blank space to record what is pending.

ACHIEVEMENTS

PENDING GOALS

In case of excess Capricorn energy, integrate Cancer energy:

- **Invite two friends to cook a meal with you.** Let everyone be involved in the process. Choose a dish you have never made. Don't follow any directions; just improvise. Don't measure the ingredients, either. "Eyeball" it. What was the result?

CAPRICORN RITUAL

MAKING MATTER SUBTLE

You will need: a pencil and a piece of paper.

1. **Think of a goal you have attained.** It could be the purpose you activated in this journal. Record everything that this achievement can bring you.

MATERIAL CONTRIBUTIONS	SPIRITUAL CONTRIBUTIONS

2. **Write the list on a piece of paper and take it into the shower with you.** As the words are washed away, feel the water performing the alchemy between the material and the spiritual.

3. **Spend ten minutes in the shower and reflect on the process.**

The future is mine for as long as I live.

JANUARY 20 - FEBRUARY 19

Element: Air of the creative network that makes space for ideas

NETWORK - CHANGE - ECCENTRICITY

AQUARIUS PROFILE

- **Ruling planet:** Uranus, god of the skies
- **Complementary opposite:** Leo, representing the necessary stars to make a constellation
- **Aligned:** Innovation, freedom, detachment
- **Off axis:** Lack of commitment, rebellion

- **Aquarius muse:**

Alicia Keys, January 25, 1981

Alicia is an Aquarian who inspires us all with her music. A classically trained pianist, she combines those skills with contemporary R&B, soul, and jazz, giving her a unique musical style. She is an artist who can "create outside the box," doesn't follow trends, and is utterly authentic.

DISSEMINATING

TAKING A LEAP OF FAITH TO FIND THE NEW

INVOKE THE ENERGY

I am an agent of constant change. My being releases the seeds of novelty. My vision foretells the future. I connect to the network by creating original bonds.

I dare to alter the pattern. My reality is open and unpredictable. I accept my distinctive features and live an authentic life. I share my freedom in the community. My challenge is to change without losing emotional contact: being down to earth and fulfilling my ideals. I make the code available so that universal information flows freely.

PHASE 11

Turn to shared creativity. Descend from the summit of your achievements. Consider new projects while you watch the results achieved. By seeing the new, you can rewrite existing patterns.

PURPOSE

- In which network are you sharing what's new?
- What unforeseen events have detoured you from what you have experienced so far?
- Is anything distracting you now?

AQUARIUS

1) Disseminating: The network is creative

★ **What if you could change the whole process, mutate it into something different, or even create it from scratch?**

Write down eleven new eccentric ideas related to your purpose.

AQUARIUS

2) Activation exercise: Alternatives

- **In a group.** Surf the internet to find a community that shares your interests. Join them.
- **As a leader.** Create your own group, blog, or profile to share your ideas.

Community name:

In case of excess Aquarius energy, integrate Leo energy:

- **Choose a day to go barefoot.** Really feel the soles of each foot in every step you take. Are you receiving the energy of the Earth?

AQUARIUS RITUAL

TELEPATHIC COMMUNICATION

You will need: an outdoor location and time.

1. Sit down comfortably in a place where you won't be interrupted.

2. Close your eyes and take some deep breaths to relax your body.

3. Think of a message you want to give the universe. Visualize the open air, the clouds, and their movements. Feel the sky listening to you.

4. Say whatever you want. Remember: only messages of love, light, and connection can be sent.

5. Now picture that thought flying away on a cloud and say goodbye to it. Refocus on your breathing and open your eyes.

PAY ATTENTION!

You will get a confirmation sign in a couple of days. Telepathy works when we are open to the universe.

PISCES

I encourage myself to experience any kind of love.

FEBRUARY 19 - MARCH 20

Element: Water as the universal source

RESONANCE - SPIRITUALITY - ART

PISCES PROFILE

- **Ruling planet:** Neptune, god of the ocean

- **Complementary opposite:** Virgo, leading to practical and material order

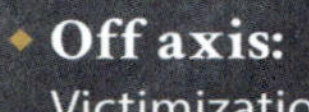

- **Aligned:** Compassion, empathy
- **Off axis:** Victimization, addiction

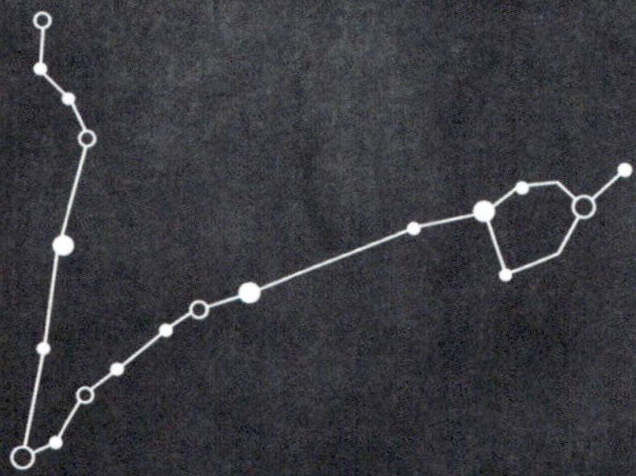

- **Pisces muse:**

Simone Biles, March 14, 1997

Simone became the most decorated gymnast in the history of the World Championships. Like any good Pisces, she has touched women around the world by telling her personal story of abuse. She has demonstrated a deep connection to her body and great insight into how to manage her exposure.

SENSITIZING

DISSOLUTION AND CONCLUSION

INVOKE THE ENERGY

I open my eyes and my world evaporates. Life flows between my fingers like sand in my hands. I dissolve form to be in touch with the whole. I transcend matter and capture the intangible. My intuition is a key that allows me to channel information. I inhabit chaos and become ethereal.

My open perception helps me surrender to immensity. I dissolve the boundaries and ego disappears so that I can love. My spirit seeks to forgive and heal. I abandon all forms of resistance. I surrender and hydrate the soil. Everything returns to the source.

PHASE 12

Dissolution of the cycle. Time to release old desires and patterns. At the end, it's essential to reabsorb what is left. It's not a material phase but rather a surrender of self. Something returns from the past to evaporate. This enables the renewal of the cycle.

PURPOSE

- What is emerging from this closure?
- What do you understand?
- What pending issues need closure?

PISCES

1) Sensitizing: Understanding

★ **Record your dreams for twelve nights.**

Every night before you go to sleep, leave this journal on your bedside table. As soon as you wake up, write down everything you remember.

To stimulate dreaming, soak your feet in salt water before going to bed or put some lavender under your pillow.

Dream 1	Dream 2	Dream 3
Dream 4	Dream 5	Dream 6
Dream 7	Dream 8	Dream 9
Dream 10	Dream 11	Dream 12

PISCES

2) Activation exercise: Flowing

- **Play some music to start the creative process. Using watercolors on a blank sheet of paper, express yourself freely.** Don't be afraid to go abstract; there are no rules to your composition. When done, take a picture of your creation and paste it here.

In case of excess Pisces energy, integrate Virgo energy:

- **Mentally take note of all the actions of your day but use only verbs.** For example: woke up, meditated, exercised, started.

PISCES RITUAL

HOLY WATER

You will need: a transparent glass, valerian or lemon balm leaves, and a rainy day.

1. On a rainy day, go out with your glass and fill it with rainwater. Don't use an umbrella or raincoat; the idea is for your body to come into contact with the rain.

2. As you fill your glass, invoke protection for yourself and those you love.

3. First thing in the morning, go outside and empty the glass on the ground, giving the water back to the earth.

CHAPTER 3

LIVING IN THE OASIS

Understanding the Cycle

CHAPTER 3

TOOLBOX

You made the journey through the desert to your purpose: welcome to the oasis. Draw here all the tools that were necessary throughout the process.

Can you find these elements in everyday life? If so, take a real toolbox and fill it with these essentials. You will then have them at hand whenever you need them.

A BALANCE OF THE TWELVE PHASES

What was your initial purpose?

Did it remain intact, or did it change throughout the process?

What phases of the journey were the most difficult for you?

What do you think were the reasons for that difficulty?

What phases did you enjoy the most?

Did they help you find any new skills?

Which people did you inspire through your process?

Who were your guides?

What are you thankful for?

What was your motto?

CONCLUDING ENERGY

It doesn't matter how you start but who you become.

1. Take note of how you are feeling after covering the twelve phases.

2. Write down three sentences that describe you today.

3. How has astrology helped you?

4. Paste your picture here when you finish the journal. Write down the date.

Date: ____________________

SUMMARIZE YOUR TWELVE PHASES

✦ **PHASE I:**

✦ **PHASE II:**

✦ **PHASE III:**

✦ **PHASE IV:**

✦ **PHASE V:**

✦ **PHASE VI:**

✦ **PHASE VII:**

✦ **PHASE VIII:**

✦ **PHASE IX:**

✦ **PHASE X:**

✦ **PHASE XI:**

✦ **PHASE XII:**

MY PROCESS AS A WRITER

My intention was to materialize my first astrology book.

- **PHASE I, ARIES, STARTING:** It all started with an intention. I wanted to make a record of the work carried out in my workshops in an astrology journal that was completely timeless.
- **PHASE II, TAURUS, MATERIALIZING:** I met with Mara and Vicky from FERA, who offered me their support. I started writing, following a content template.
- **PHASE III, GEMINI, CONNECTING:** I wrote down ideas. I asked my friends for suggestions for the content. I looked for the available material and added new elements.
- **PHASE IV, CANCER, CONTAINING:** I spent day and night writing. I had to feed the body of this book project.
- **PHASE V, LEO, CREATING:** After lots of hard work, my personal style started to appear. I posted about this on social media. I put myself out there. (This is one of the phases I find the hardest!)
- **PHASE VI, VIRGO, ANALYZING:** I returned to the template. I adjusted, corrected, reviewed. It was the time for the technicalities and formalities required by the contract.
- **PHASE VII, LIBRA, HARMONIZING:** I considered who this journal was aimed at. There were conversations with the editors about aesthetics and ways of communicating the content.
- **PHASE VIII, SCORPIO, DEEPENING:** Everything blew up. I fell into a crisis. I lost myself. I was tired and questioning the whole process. I suffered from writer's block.
- **PHASE IX, SAGITTARIUS, UNDERSTANDING:** I revisited the idea of taking a trip. I made up my mind to buy plane tickets and unblock the process. Inspiration returned. I went from ideal to real.
- **PHASE X, CAPRICORN, STRUCTURING:** I submitted the book for printing.
- **PHASE XI, AQUARIUS, DISSEMINATING:** Internet circulation. Time to share and change my communication on social media. The book has a life of its own. I am already thinking of what's next!
- **PHASE XII, PISCES, SENSITIZING:** I arrived at the oasis! This journal inspires many people, transcending me. I surrender it to humanity.

ABOUT THE AUTHOR

Agustina Malter Terrada, born in Argentina, has worked as an astrologer since 2012. She offers workshops, natal chart readings, and active research. She currently resides in Spain.

I love writing and choosing inspiring images.
*I am a **Gemini** with Pisces rising. Words are my art and medicine. I share magic in my temple: @astrologiaparamar.*

Based on the symbolism of the wheel, **Red Wheel** offers books and divination decks from a variety of traditions. We aim to provide the ideas, information, and innovative approaches to help you develop your own spiritual path.

Please visit our website
www.redwheelweiser.com
to learn more about our
full range of titles.